startingout orstartingover

Living Your Best Life

Ms Melissa J. Stack

ISBN: 0988554704
ISBN-13: 9780988554702

Library of Congress Control Number: 2013906976
CreateSpace Independent Publishing Platform
North Charleston, South Carolina

Dedication

To my husband, Bill, who makes me believe I can do anything.
To Billy and Sammy, who gave me the chance to be a parent—I love you both.
For my nieces and nephews—may your lives be blessed beyond your wildest dreams!
To my parents—most of what I know came from you.

Contents

"No matter what the level of your ability, you have more potential than you can ever develop in a lifetime."

James T. McCay

Getting Started

Think of this book as a primer. Remember those from grade school? They didn't teach you everything you needed to know about reading—they got you started. This book is a primer about life. It represents twenty-eight important ideas to keep in mind as you experience life. It is written in an article format, and each "article" ends with at least one action you can take to get started in living a better life. In addition, wherever possible, I have recommended books that may help you learn more about a subject.

The book represents ideas that I have learned over my first fifty years of life. Some of that learning happened the hard way through experience. Some if it I learned through reading and learning from others. My first fifty years have been great; I consider myself fortunate to have the experiences and blessings I have had so far.

The catalyst for writing this book and sharing these ideas was that many of the lessons I learned later in life, and many I wish I had learned earlier. My goal is to share those ideas with you, the reader, and it is my sincerest hope that there are ideas in this book that you will want to start doing right away. If you are just starting out, they will help you build a successful life from the start. On the other hand, if you are at a place where you think you need to "start over," they can be equally helpful. It is never too late to start living a better life.

I hope that all the articles are helpful, but I realize that not all of them may apply to everyone in every situation. As they say in Al-Anon, take what you like, and leave the rest. May this book be one of the ways that help you start your journey to a better life!

Enjoy!

Go After Your Dreams

I am a high achiever, setting the bar high and then going after it. Two years ago, I dared to set what author Jim Collins calls a BHAG: Big Hairy Audacious Goal! That goal was to become a writer. What have I accomplished so far? I have started a blog, written more than ninety articles, dared to have an editor review my writing, and took the steps to get my book published. I wouldn't have taken any of these actions if I didn't have a dream, a goal that I had to achieve.

Going after your dreams can be one of the scariest and best things you will ever do. Most of the great companies, novels written, and new gadgets, all started from a dream. Everyone should have dreams and take steps toward achieving them. Life is short and not meant to be lived timidly. The world may be waiting for the gift you have to offer, so go after your dreams because you are here to do something unique and special. You will never know what your gift is until you start to make your dreams and ideas come alive.

In giving flight to a dream, there are a few things to keep in mind.

First, it isn't easy to go after your dreams. Although taking that first step might be the hardest, the next million or so don't seem to get any easier. Like the Winter Warlock says in *Santa Claus Is Coming to Town*, "You have to put one foot in front of the other" and then repeat many, many times. Although it is not easy, there can be many surprising benefits that come as a result of taking action toward your dream. No matter how hard it may seem at the moment, it is important not to give up too easily. Dreams worth going after are worth working toward.

The second lesson is to build your confidence and belief in yourself. For me, confidence was an issue before I started on this project. The more I continue to go after my dream and try things I am afraid to do, the more confidence I build. I know from reading stories of successful people that the common thread is their belief in their ideas regardless of how many people reject or don't believe in their dream. Take Walt Disney. In the beginning, no one believed in a cartoonist with a mouse as a main character, but he kept believing and working toward his dream. He believed in himself.

The third lesson is that "a setback can be a set up for a comeback," as author Willie Jolley says. Like many of you, I am not good at failure or disappointment. As a high achiever, I have spent a lifetime trying to get it right, on the first try. Going after your dreams pulls you in what feels like the opposite direction. It is hard to fail and learn to "dust yourself off" and move on. Think about actors or comedians and their ability to "hang in there." Think about their resolve to take many NO's before they get one yes. Continuing to dust yourself off and move forward is one of the most distinguishing factors between success and failure. It is important to remember that if it was easy to reach for the stars, everyone would do it. Only a few do, because it is hard work and takes a lot of perseverance.

The fourth lesson is recognizing how short life is. When you are young and have your whole life ahead of you, it seems as if time is endless. The world is your oyster, so if you don't start working on your dreams right away, that is okay, because you know you have plenty of time to start later. We don't know how long we will be here on the earth. The good news is that most of us live long lives with plenty of time to work on our dreams, but you don't know. What if your dream could help others, make a difference in their lives or the world? It can't if you don't start on it. We are all here on earth for a unique purpose. We need to get started on our purpose as quickly as possible. Life is too short not to challenge ourselves to become what we were created to be.

The fifth lesson is perseverance. As the saying goes, "All good things come to those who wait." We live in an instantaneous world. We measure wait times in seconds. We get frustrated if it takes a minute for a computer to process a command. The fast pace and need for instant gratification go against the effort and time it takes to achieve our dreams. Athletes do not develop skill and ability overnight. Even the great, talented Michael Jordan or Tom Brady was not immediately successful at achieving his dreams or developing his skills. "Practice, practice, practice" or "try, try, try" are the mottos for achieving your dreams.

As a recap, here are five important ideas to remember in reaching for your dreams:

1. Take one step after another toward your dream.
2. Develop confidence and believe in yourself.

3. Setbacks are stepping stones toward reaching your goals.
4. Life is short, so start working on your dreams now.
5. Persevere—keep moving in the direction of your dreams.

Today, think about your dreams. What are they? What actions can you take to reach them? Start making a list of all the ideas and dreams you have. Decide, this week, to take one step toward your dream.

Go After Your Dreams Quiz

What are your dreams? Use this page to capture your dream list.

1. ______________________________

2. ______________________________

3. ______________________________

4. ______________________________

5. ______________________________

6. ______________________________

7. ______________________________

8. ______________________________

9. ______________________________

10. ______________________________

11. ______________________________

12. ______________________________

13. ______________________________

14. ______________________________

15. ____

16. ____

17. ____

18. ____

19. ____

20. ____

Grow Your Confidence Muscle

I caught your attention with the idea of a dream, but now you need to think about the confidence it will take to go after it or to make changes in your life. You may ask yourself, "What if I am not confident? Can I learn to be confident?" I believe you can. It's like learning to develop a muscle. Before you exercise that muscle, it doesn't appear it will be able to do much of anything, but the more you practice and build your strength, the more that muscle can do. It is the same with growing your confidence. To develop a stronger sense of confidence, you are going to have to do some things differently.

The book *What's Holding You Back* by Sam Horn is an excellent resource to help you understand more about confidence, assess what might be getting in your way, and take concrete steps toward raising your confidence.

There are four areas where you may habitually sabotage yourself. As you read, consider if there is an area you need to focus on.

Carry Yourself Positively

How you carry yourself sends an immediate message to others. The way you stand or speak often gives others a louder message than any words could. Consider what messages you are sending by answering the following questions.

- How do you present yourself (physically, how you dress) to the world? Write down how others might perceive you.
- Do you look people in the eye? What types of words do you use?
- What does the way you dress say to others?

Talk to Yourself

According to the National Science Foundation, the average person has between 12,000 and 50,000 thoughts a day. These thoughts are often in the form of audible words we tell ourselves. Unfortunately, many of us do not spend a lot of time sending positive messages. Visualization—a technique used by many athletes—is when a person forms a mental picture of achieving a desired goal and talks to himself or herself in a positive manner. According to Psychology Today, the research has shown that visualization can be equal to physical practice in helping an athlete to be successful. So if what you say to yourself or "how see yourself " can have an affect on your actual performance, then you need to be very careful about what scenarios you play in your head. Take a moment and think about: What messages are you telling yourself? How would you describe yourself? What words do you say about yourself in your head or out loud? What pictures are you creating in your mind?

It's time to take inventory of your thoughts and stop any that are not moving you in a positive direction.

Live in the Present

Many of us have had bad breaks, disappointments, and painful experiences. These can often paralyze us and cause us to shut down. However, many people who have achieved the greatest success have had to overcome setbacks, negativity, and rejection. The great Thomas Edison had a teacher who said that he was "addled" or stupid as recounted in the book on Thomas Edison by Charles Pederson. Edison and others who succeeded chose to leave those bad experiences and memories where they belonged—in the past. They approached each new day as an opportunity in which the past did not dictate or influence. If you continue to relive the past, you rob yourself of your present and future potential.

- Are your thoughts focused on today and the future, or do you tend to recall and relive past, negative events?
- What success stories do you have? What achievements have you made?
- What are you good at? What makes you unique?

Take the Driver's Seat

As an adult, you have the pleasure of having responsibility over your life. There may be others who influence the choices you make, but in the end, you are in control of your life. You are where you are today because of the decisions *you* made or allowed others to make for you.

- Are you spending time working on what you want?
- Do you express your thoughts even when others disagree?
- How often do you allow yourself to say "no" to others' requests?
- Do you speak up when your rights or needs are being violated?

The Little-Known Courage Muscle

Many of us incorrectly believe that we have to have courage before we can take action. It is the other way around. By facing your fears and overcoming them with action, you create your own confidence. Sometimes it helps to have someone cheering and assisting you on the road to success. Get a coach—it works for athletes and is gaining popularity in business. Having help may be an important step in being successful, but remember that ultimately you are the one who has to take action, run the race, and overcome the obstacles. The more determined you are, the better able you are to reach the more difficult targets. Susan Jeffers, author of Feel the Fear and Do It Anyways, says it well: "Feel the fear and do it anyway."

- What actions have you taken recently even though you were afraid?
- What actions didn't you take because of fear?
- Who is your role model of confidence? What actions does this person take that lead you to believe he or she is confidence?

What areas do you need to concentrate on to become more confident? Today, commit to taking at least one action to move you toward being more confident. Start by answering the questions above, or do something that you have been putting off. Action is the exercise that builds your confidence muscle.

Grow Your Confidence Muscle Quiz

The questions below help you evaluate where to focus to build your confidence.

What is your physical appearance saying to the world? Do you dress appropriately? Are your clothes neat and taken care of? Do your hair and makeup send the message you want to send?

____

____

____

____

Many of us talk to ourselves, but most of the messages are negative and self-destructive. To become more confident, we need to learn to speak to ourselves positively and appreciate our skills and uniqueness. Write down five positive qualities about yourself.

1. ____________________________________

2. ____________________________________

3. ____________________________________

4. ____________________________________

5. ____________________________________

All of us have success stories. Those who are more positive and confident remember and use past successes to build on them in the future. What are some of your best success stories?

1. ____

2. ____

3. ____

4. ____

5. ____

Start Everything with a Goal

It started as a suggestion in Melody Beattie's book, *Gratitude: Affirming the Good Things in Life*. Beattie suggests writing down every dream and wish you have then turning it into a goal. At that point in my life, I needed motivation and didn't have anything to lose, so I bought a notebook and started to write.

Every time I heard myself say, "I wish," I wrote it in my notebook. I added to the list and reread it often. One item on the list stood out as an impossible wish: saving $10,000. At the time, it might as well have been a million dollars, because I had no idea how I was going to achieve it. I read that goal every week, and I started to think a lot about it. I started to make some changes. I closed a Visa account with a balance that never seemed to decrease. I started increasing the amount taken out of my paycheck and put it into savings. Lo and behold, over time I had saved $10,000! I was shocked. Even more shocking was that as I looked at my list, I realized that I had started achieving other goals as well. As I completed a goal, I moved it to a "Completed" list with the date accomplished. That was nine years ago.

Since starting that exercise, I added a few other steps but continue to keep it simple and make progress. Today, I write a list of goals every day until I fill the page of my notebook. Once a month, I move any new goals to my running list of uncompleted goals and continue to keep track of those I accomplish. By writing down my goals, I've been able to complete more than I ever imagined—even traveling to Australia!

Today, take out a piece of paper, and write down every dream and wish you have, whether big or small. As new ideas come to you, add them to the list. Do this for six months—you will do it for a lifetime once you see what begins to happen. If you want to learn more about the importance of goals, read Brian Tracy's book, *Goals*.

Start Everything with a Goal

What are your goals for this year? Start by defining your overall mission. If you are not sure what that is, that's okay. You can come back to that later. What is critical is to start the practice of identifying and writing out your goals. Below write your top ten goals personally and professionally. Refer back to this list regularly and watch what happens.

Top Ten Professional/Business Goals	
My overall professional goal/mission:	
1	
2	
3	
4	
5	
6	
7	
8	
9	
10	

Top Ten Personal Goals	
My overall life goal/mission:	
1	
2	
3	
4	
5	
6	
7	
8	
9	
10	

Use Good Manners

One day last week, my boss didn't notice that I was in the office all day. In the same week, I broke one of my own rules: I answered a call on my cellphone when I was meeting with someone in my office. Finally, my son was relying a story of his friend who thought it was appropriate to text a girl that he just met twenty times in one hour. What do these situations have in common? They are all evidence of our need to act with good manners. With the changes in technology, especially cellphones and computers, more focus on self-gratification, and the increased need for instant gratification, we need to make sure that we are balancing these with good manners.

I have noticed a change and, in many cases, a decrease in good manners. How many of us have experienced an individual having a private phone conversation in a public place or have been concerned with a driver's ability and knew that he or she was talking or texting while trying to drive? The need for good manners has been a popular subject for many years. For years, Emily Post was the expert on this important subject, but it may surprise you to learn that George Washington wrote about good manners in the 1700s. At the age of sixteen, he wrote *Rules of Civility & Decent Behavior in Company and Conversation: A Book of Etiquette.* In it, Washington developed 110 rules for good manners. Interestingly, many of them are applicable today.

1. Every action done in Company ought be with some sign of respect, to those that are present.
2. Sleep not when others speak.
3. Read no Letters, Book or Papers in company, but when there is a necessity for doing of it you must ask leave.[1]

What are good manners or civility, anyway? It is making sure that our words and actions convey a sense of respect, care, and consideration for the people with whom we come in contact.

Reader's Digest did a survey in 2006 to see if people were courteous throughout the world. Surprisingly, New York City ranked the highest in terms of courtesy, contrary to what many may think about that city. In one of the places where they conducted their experiments, a Starbucks coffee shop, the researchers were told by the frontline staff that they were taught to be courteous as part of their training.

Why are good manners so important? Most of us don't like being treated rudely or disregarded. yet how many of us have forgotten The Golden Rule: Treat others as you would like to be treated.

Wikihow.com and other websites have many suggestions on etiquette. Based on what I notice on a daily basis, I think there are rights that everyone should have related to courtesy and treating individuals with respect.

---

1 George Washington, *Rules of Civility & Decent Behavior in Company and Conversation: A Book of Etiquette* (Washington, DC: W.H. Morrison, 1888) p.15.

Ten Rules of Civility

1. See people as people first. This means recognizing them as individuals before you look at them as workers, servers, and other service personnel. This also means treating them with courtesy and recognition.
2. Use polite phrases often. Say "good morning," "please," "thank you," and "you're welcome."
3. Pay attention to how you carry yourself. It makes a statement about whether or not you respect yourself and others. This means being aware of your dress. Going to a nice restaurant, a wedding, or a funeral and not dressing appropriately is disrespectful to others.
4. Exercise good driving manners. This is not only a courtesy issue; it is a safety issue. Driving is an activity in which you must be alert and looking out for dangerous situations. You can't do that when you concentrate on what you are saying on a cellphone or texting someone.
5. Think before you speak. Over the years, we have become more comfortable with stating our opinions, standing up for our rights, and questioning authority. Nowhere does it say that it is okay to be rude, spiteful, and deliberately hurtful to make a point. You can state your opinion, disagree, or question without acting boorishly.
6. Respect authority. This includes parents, elders, police, politicians, teachers, and others. I am saddened that we as viewers are not outraged by the behavior of some of our TV journalists. It is okay to disagree with the president; it is not okay to disrespect who he is and the office he holds. This type of behavior also disrespects the profession of journalism, the TV station the journalists work for, and the American people.

7. Be kind even when others don't appear to deserve it. Acting in the same manner as others may escalate an issue. You can decide to be an example of better behavior.
8. Be a good listener. Most of us want others to pay attention to us. It is important that we learn to slow down so that we can truly hear what others are saying. Doing so may provide clarity and understanding as well as showing care and respect. Those who are good listeners are sought after as being individuals who make others feel important and valued.
9. Be timely. In our overcharged world, many of us are overbooked. We hate it when we have to wait at the doctor's office, because we think it is a sign of a lack of respect for our time, but many of us are guilty of making others wait and supplying excuses for why it happened. We need to make sure that we are not conveying an air of superiority. Regardless of title, everyone's time is important, and we should respect that.
10. Be a role model. This is the hardest, and the best, way to show respect. What do our daily actions convey? Are we showing positive intent toward others or acting in ways that show disregard? Remember that we may influence others to emulate our behavior. Are we acting in the ways we would like others to act?

We all need a code of conduct. What is yours, and how are you measuring up to it? Are there areas you need to focus on to become a person who is a role model of courtesy and good manners? Determine one area that you need to focus on, and start making changes today—others will appreciate the change.

Use Good Manners Quiz

Most of us are quick to give ourselves high marks for good manners but are quick to identify where others need to improve. Take this short self-assessment to pinpoint what you need to focus on to improve the perception others have of you or improve your personal and profession relationships.

	Behavior	Hardly ever	Make an effort but not consistent
1	Do you see people first and their profession second?		
2	Do you use polite phrases often (please, thank you)?		
3	Do you carry yourself appropriately (dress appropriately for the occasions, take care of your appearance and clothing, carry yourself positively)?		
4	Do you exercise good manners when driving?		
5	Do you think before you speak?		
6	Do you respect authority even when you don't agree?		
7	Are you kind?		
8	Are you a good listener?		
9	Do you get to meetings and appointments on time? Do you complete work on time and meet deadlines?		
10	Are you a role model of good manners?		

Use Good Manners

Act positively more than 50 percent of the time	Consciously think about the right behavior and act positively most of the time	Role model for this behavior

Laugh

Do you know what Patch Adams and Norman Cousins have in common? Both believed in the power of laughter. Patch Adams's fascinating life story includes the uncommon road he took to become a doctor who literally believed that laughter was the best medicine. Norman Cousins wrote *Anatomy of Illness* after he cured himself through laughter. I learned the importance of laughter from my mother. She taught us early on that if given a choice in any circumstance, choose laughter. She encouraged us to laugh on a daily basis and thought that the best thing was to laugh until you cried.

As a child, it amazed me how much my mother laughed, especially given her childhood experiences. After her mother died when she was two, she went to live with relatives and ended up also losing these important parental figures early in life, but to despite these difficulties, my mother saw the importance of humor and instilled in us ability to laugh.

Life is serious business, but that doesn't mean that we need to take ourselves seriously all the time. There's plenty in this world that can get us down or make us worry. These are the times when laughter is most important.

However, it's not just the happy attitude we feel while laughing that causes us relief; there is a physical aspect. Laughter releases endorphins, natural painkillers; while at the same time suppresses levels of epinephrine, which is a stress hormone (Scientific American, 2011). Most of the things we worry about or lose sleep over will not be significant in the long run, and if that's the case, we do not need to spend a lot of energy on them now. Any time you spend worrying or being stressed releases epinephrine, which can affect your long-term health.

Make a commitment to have a new outlook on life. Adopt new habits: watch one funny movie a week (start with *Patch Adams* starring Robin Williams), learn to smile more, and see the humor in more situations. Make it a goal to do something once a day to make yourself laugh by looking at cartoons, learning a funny joke, or seeing the humor in your own situation. As the saying goes, "It is not what happens to you, it's what you do with what happens to you" that makes a difference in the quality of your life. Decide today to impact someone's life every day by adding a little cheer, and notice how much better *you* feel.

Laugh Yourself to Good Health List

Here is a list of some of the funniest movies of all times. How many have you already seen? Make a commitment to see at least one funny movie each month. Highlight the movies you will watch this coming year.

	Movie	Already Seen It	On My List for This Year
1	*The Hangover*		
2	*Animal House*		
3	*Beverly Hills Cop*		
4	*Groundhog Day*		
5	*The 40 Year Old Virgin*		
6	*Blazing Saddles*		
7	*Anchorman: The Legend of Ron Burgundy*		
8	*Talladega Nights*		
9	*Role Models*		
10	*The Jerk*		
11	*National Lampoon's Vacation*		
12	*Caddy Shack*		
13	*Raising Arizona*		
14	*Young Frankenstein*		
15	*Monty Python and the Holy Grail*		
16	*Airplane*		
17	*9 to 5*		
18	*Arthur*		
19	*Bridesmaids*		
20	*Dumb and Dumber*		

21	*Planes, Trains, and Automobiles*		
22	*There's Something about Mary*		
23	*Trading Places*		
24	*Step Brothers*		
25	*Wedding Crashers*		
26	*Wayne's World*		
27	*National Lampoon's Christmas Vacation*		
28	*Office Spaces*		

Take Care of Yourself

Recently, we had a party for my mother's seventieth birthday. During the occasion, I was trying to convince my siblings about the importance of capturing a picture of all of us. While moaning, one of my sisters complained, "Do we have to? I am suffering from a decade of bad hair days." I laughed, but I also felt sad. My sister is a pretty woman who doesn't seem to play up or focus on her own beauty. As I thought about it, I wondered why she didn't spend more time focusing on herself. I think that like many mothers, she has many demands from children, a husband, and other responsibilities.

If you fly, you have heard the flight attendant tell you that if it becomes necessary to use an oxygen mask, that you should place it on you first, then help others. The same rule should apply to taking care of yourself. You need to take care of you first, if you are going to help others and be a good role model for your children.

There is mounting research on how important taking care of yourself is to your overall health, serenity, and ability to handle stress. Yet, many women are overweight and do little or no leisure activities. Taking care of ourselves should not be seen as a luxury but an essential part of being healthy, the same way that we know about the importance of eating the right foods to stay healthy.

What are some tips to start in a new direction and learn to take better care of yourself:

Take a break every day. If this seems impossible, start small. A five-minute break is better than no break. There is research showing that to stay creative, the mind needs a break every forty-five minutes. Our bodies need a break from continuous activity. If you are working outside the home, do you take a fifteen-minute break during the day? Make a commitment to take a break of five to fifteen minutes on a daily basis. Use this time to have a cup of tea, take a quick walk, or do nothing. Determine what amount of time you can commit to daily, and start doing it.

Keep up with your hobbies and interests. Taking the time to do something that you thoroughly enjoy has many benefits. It gives you the chance to recharge and your mind to relax. Experience doing something just for the joy and pleasure of it. For me, that activity is sewing, and I make sure that I sew a couple of times a week even if it's only for ten minutes at a time. I have to concentrate to sew, which means, by default, that I can't think about other things. This gives my mind the chance to unwind. It also brings me joy. It allows me to be express my creativity, which is an important part of who I am. A hobby doesn't have to be creating something. It can be listening to music, seeing a movie, or walking in nature. Make a list of the things you love to do, and start doing them more often.

Learn to say "no." I think this might be one of the hardest words to learn, especially for women. I was listening to a CD yesterday in which David Heinemeier Hansson talked about the importance of focusing on doing a few things well versus trying to do everything. We all have a finite amount of time every day; so we need to make sure that important activities and commitments are not being squeezed out by the noise of unimportant tasks and activities. Do you have trouble saying no in general or only around certain people or causes? Once you determine where you need to increase the number of No's, make it a game of it. Like exercising, start small. Make a commitment to say no to something once a day, and work to increase the frequency. Learn to recognize the unimportant and the requests that conflict with your own goals, and start saying no.

Ask for help when you need it. When I was two, I told my mother that "I would do it myself," and that has been my motto ever since. I know how difficult it can be to ask for help, but we all need help. If you find you are frustrated by the lack of help, figure out if you are being direct enough and if others know what is expected. My husband is always reminding me that I should ask for his help and not assume that he intuitively knows I need it. Seek help by sharing. You may find that others have a solution that works for you.

Pay attention to your spiritual life. Whatever your belief is, honor it. Maybe it is a support group, a prayer group, or a weekly church service. Make it a frequent habit. For me, this practice includes daily reading from a spiritual writing and a moment of prayer. Over the years, it has become as needed as brushing my teeth. We need to spend some of our energy connecting with a power greater than ourselves, however you have defined that power.

Good food, exercise, and sleep. We all know the importance of eating right and lowering the amount of saturated fat, sugar, and low-nutrition foods from our diet. We probably know that what we eat affects our mood, mental alertness, and health. We are probably aware of the importance of making exercise a part of our weekly routine, and all the weight-loss shows endorse exercise. The third part of this equation is getting enough sleep. It is scary how sleep deprived we are becoming as a nation. Each of us needs a certain amount of sleep for our bodies to function well and our brains to work effectively. For most of us, we need seven to eight hours of sleep, yet many of us do not get this amount on a regular basis. The effects of sleep deprivation are more severe than just being edgy the next day. Continuously getting less sleep than is required can have negative effects on your heart. If you need to get more sleep, start by going to bed fifteen minutes earlier than normal and slowly increase this increment.

Stop comparing yourself to others, and start focusing on your gifts and talents. Comparing ourselves to others is at best a waste of energy and at worst a form of self-sabotage. Every one of us can find someone who is thinner, makes more money, or is more "put together." These comparisons don't help us get better; they zap our energy and make us focus on the wrong things. Spend your energy thinking about what makes you unique. What do you bring to the world that no one else can? Make a list. Add to the list. Ask others what they see, and use that list as a daily remainder to focus your energy on being good to yourself.

For some of us, learning to take care of ourselves may feel selfish. Learn to let go of that feeling. It may mean that we need to learn about what we like, what makes us unique, and how to relax. Thomas Edison worked long hours on his inventions, but he also credited naps for some of his breakthrough inventions. Make a commitment to yourself, for yourself, to start doing at least one thing from this list. You are worth it. Learn to take good care of yourself.

Take Care of Yourself Quiz

Living a better life starts with taking care of yourself. Read each statement below, and give yourself a point for every statement that reflects an action you take regularly.

1. I regularly take breaks during the day. I get up from my desk (if I sit at one) and stretch my legs. I take a lunch break most days. ________

2. I spend fifteen to thirty minutes a day doing an activity or hobby that I enjoy. ________

3. I get enough sleep on a regular basis. ________

4. I exercise at least thirty minutes three to four times a week. ________

5. I don't overcommit myself. I say "no" to invites and requests that take me away from my priorities. ________

6. I spend some time each week relaxing. ________

7. I pay attention to my spiritual needs regularly. ________

8. I focus my attention on me. I minimize thoughts that involve comparing myself to others. ________

9. I put myself first by making a choice to take care of myself, physically and mentally. ________

10. I take time, on a regular basis, to cultivate friendships and connect with others. ________

Are there areas of your life that need attention? Are there aspects that you should make changes in?

____

____

____

____

Be Successful with Your Money

My first experience in learning to save money started with my first job, babysitting, at the age of fourteen. Most of the money I earned went directly into my savings account. Although it seemed the wise thing to do, I didn't realize until much later how much this decision guided me toward financial success. Unfortunately, I didn't learn many of the other important lessons until I was much older. As I reflect on the financial habits of my youth, I wish that someone had taken the time to point me in the right direction sooner. The effect would have been less debt, more saving, and more wealth building.

Financial health often requires as much attention as it takes to be physically healthy. Given our recent economic crisis and the high unemployment rate, we all need to focus on our financial practices. How confident are you that you could handle a financial emergency? Are you saving toward your retirement? Are you getting by only by using credit cards? You may feel good about your finances, but how do you know if you are taking the right steps to ensure that you have a healthy financial future?

My road to building financial security was rocky and undisciplined. As a result, I made a lot of mistakes. Through these mistakes and with the help of good finance books, I learned some simple steps that have made a sizable difference in my ability to create savings and pay off debt.

These "starter" steps" can help you create a better financial future.

1. **Save 10 percent of everything you make.** This is often a difficult rule to follow. One way to get started is to set up an automatic transfer that comes out of your paycheck or bank account and goes into some type of savings account. The savings account may be with your local bank, or you may find that setting up a mutual fund makes more sense. Make it a goal to save 10 percent of all your income including bonuses, special payments, and other irregular, nonsalary monies. You will be amazed by how quickly this adds up.

2. **Pay off your credit card balance every month**. Do you know that the average American has more than $8,000 in credit card debt? If you are carrying a credit card balance every month, it is time to go on a credit card diet. Decide to stop using your credit card and begin paying down the balance. Get into a habit of paying cash. If you don't have the cash, don't buy it. Once your credit card balance is zero, discipline yourself to pay off any balance each month. Don't put more on your card than you can pay off that month. Even better, learn to use your credit card only for true emergencies.

3. **Save for large purchases**. Rather than make payments on expensive purchases, use different savings accounts that are earmarked for big purchases. Have a car account, a furniture account, and a vacation account, to name a few. Systemati-

cally fund these accounts by having money transferred into them each month from your savings account. Instead of making a car payment to a dealership, put the money in the car fund. Little by little, the account grows until you have enough to buy your new car with cash. This same principle can be used for vacations, furniture, or just about anything.

4. **Track your inflows and outflows of money.** Most people would be shocked to see where their money goes as a result of unconscious spending. It's important to know where your money is going. One of the best tools to help you do this is Quicken®. By tracking expenses, you can determine if you need to make changes in your spending habits. It can also make budgeting and taxes preparation much easier and less time consuming.

5. **Invest in a retirement plan.** Ideally, you work for a company that provides this as a benefit to employees. If not, start saving on your own. With costs continuing to rise, Medicare and Social Security in trouble, and company pensions becoming extinct, it is important that we all start funding our own retirements. This is often something we view as far into the future—until we are suddenly facing retirement and realize that we have nothing to get us through it. The longer you are saving for a retirement, the better. Start with your first job.

6. **Start an emergency fund.** Financial advisor and author Dave Ramsey talks about the importance of planning for "Murphy's Law." Murphy's Law is the phenomenon that unfortunate things always seem to happen at the worst times. You need new tires when you have no extra money. The hot water heater needs to be replaced at Christmas time, or the insurance bill comes right after you book a vacation. These surprise

expenses tend can destroy your budget and often come when you don't have any extra money. An emergency fund is a way to plan for unforeseen events ahead of time. How much you will need depends upon your personal circumstances, but a good starting place is $1,000 to $2,000.

7. **Protect your assets and family**. Make sure that you have adequate insurance (medical, home, auto, life, and disability). As much as most of us don't want to think about something bad happening, it can. One out of four adults will need disability insurance in their lifetime (Social Security Administration, 2011). Although you may hope that you will never need this safety net, proper coverage can help protect you financially if something unfortunate happens.

8. **Set financial goals and become educated about money.** The average working person is going to make at least $1 million in his or her lifetime (US Census Bureau, 2011). How much will you have saved or invested? Part of being financially healthy is setting goals for saving and funding your goals, whether that is a house, a van, or travel. Educate yourself to make good investment choices. There are many books and resources to help you. Two great books to start with are *Total Money Makeover* by Dave Ramsey and *The Wealthy Barber* by David Chilton.

How healthy are you financially? Take the quiz on the next page. If you score below 23, decide on the areas where you want to make changes. Make a commitment to yourself to make one change this year. You will be positively surprised how much change you see in one year.

FINANCIAL HEALTH QUIZ

Read each of the questions and circle the answer that best represents where you are financially. Be honest.

		A 0 points	B 1 point	C 2 points	D 3 points
1	I invest the following percent on a regular basis toward my retirement.	0–3%	4–7%	8–10%	10%+
2	I have a credit card balance.	> $4,000	< $4,000	< $2,000	$0
3	I save for large purchases like a car, TV, or vacation.	Rarely	Sometimes	Often	Always
4	I track my inflow and outflow of money. I can tell you by category where I spend my money.	Rarely	Sometimes	Often	Always
5	I save __ percent of my money.	0–3%	4–7%	8–10%	10%+
6	I have at an emergency fund so that I can pay for unforeseen expenses. I maintain an emergency fund of:	$0	$500	$1,000	$1,500+
7	I use a monthly budget to ensure that I have a plan for my money and don't waste it.	Rarely	Sometimes	Often	Always
8	I set financial goals on a regular basis.	Rarely	Sometimes	Often	Always
9	I learn about finances by reading magazines like *Money* or books like *Total Money Makeover* on a regular basis.	Hardly Ever	Annually	Quarterly	Monthly

	Score Total Points for each tem Circled in each Column				

Overall Score:

Score

23–27	Excellent	You are doing well at the basics of financial health. Continue to learn about money, and figure out what additional steps you can take to ensure that you have a solid financial future.
19–22	Good	You are taking several of the steps you need to ensure that you have a solid financial future. Focus on the specific changes needed to increase your financial health.
14–18	Need to make some changes	Although you are taking some steps to ensure a solid financial future, you are doing so inconsistently. Figure out what is getting in the way, and make a plan to overcome any obstacles.
<14	Money crisis	Your financial health is in serious jeopardy. Take a look at where there are gaps, and make lifestyle changes as soon as possible.

My Short-Term Financial Goals

1. ____

2. ____

3. ____

How to Become a Lucky Person

I truly believe there are people who are lucky. You know the ones; they can go into a casino and win. I have a friend like that, and she appears to be naturally lucky, or is she? I know she is willing to spend more money at the blackjack table than I ever would. Is she lucky, or does she increase her odds of winning by the amount of money she is willing to lose?

Over the last couple of years, I have known many individuals who have been affected by the economy and lost their jobs. Many times, the circumstances are not within their control, but that doesn't seem to help with the feeling of loss that it brings. It can be difficult to feel lucky or upbeat when you have the stress of bills and obligations.

I am a worrier, which means that if I don't have something legitimate to worry about, I can find new or future events to stress over. The more I worry, the more fearful or depressed I become. Although I have become better over the years, I still find that I am concerned that something "bad" might happen in the future and affect my job, health, or family.

Do lucky people exist, and can you become one of them? According to author Richard Wiseman, the answer is yes. He studied what makes some people lucky and others not, and he discovered that lucky people think and behave in different ways. These differences create good fortune in their life.

Wiseman discovered four principles that separate lucky people from others. Some of the key attributes of individuals who appear lucky include their outlook on life. They expect good fortune. They are open to possibility. They see themselves as having more control over events, and therefore, they are able to make their own luck.

If like me, you want to turn over a new leaf and feel luckier, what do you need to do differently? The first step is to be more open to new experiences. Rather than get caught up in routine, lucky individuals are looking for and open to new experiences. They are willing to take risks. Another way that lucky people operate differently is they trust their "gut" and act on this stored knowledge. Lucky people tend to process events differently. The ability to see something as positive or negative has an effect on the ideas that they generate. The more positive the reaction, the better the solutions they generate.

What are some things that we can do to make our own luck and see ourselves as lucky people? Wiseman has four principles that he believes help to create good fortune in your life and career.

1. Maximize chance opportunities. Lucky people are on the lookout for what the rest of us would call "chance opportunities." They not only notice them, they also create them or act on them. They tend to be well connected, relaxed, and open to new experiences. Ask yourself, "How can I become more open to new experiences?"

2. They listen to their gut. Lucky people hone their skills in recognizing what their gut is suggesting and acting on it.
3. Expect good fortune. Lucky people are certain that the future will be bright, and this belief turns into reality. They create a positive future.
4. They don't accept bad luck as a permanent condition and tend to turn it into a good, sometimes just by recognizing that it could have been worse. Rather than letting the situation control them, they take control of the situation.

Here's a step you can take today to start on a new path and think like a lucky person. Start keeping a "lucky diary." This is a technique that Wiseman uses in his "Luck School" training classes and it is simple. At the end of the day, write down the positive and lucky things that happened to you. Do not write any unlucky stuff. Wiseman recommends doing this for at least a month, and see if you notice more positive and lucky things happening in your life.

Another way to let go of worrying is by scheduling it. Help your mind learn to worry less by forcing it to think worried thoughts only during certain times of the day. Allow three minutes of worrying three times a day, and see if this slows down the amount of worrisome thoughts you have.

If you want to learn more about Wiseman's work, read *The Luck Factor: Changing Your Luck, Changing Your Life: The Four Essential Principles*.

Taking Chances

If learning to be lucky involves new experiences, we need to learn to recognize those opportunities. Write 10 past experiences that you think were a result of "chance or good fortunate". Then write what you did or thought that helped you seize the opportunity.

	Lucky Experiences	Thought/Action You Took
1.	______________________	______________________
2.	______________________	______________________
3.	______________________	______________________
4.	______________________	______________________
5.	______________________	______________________
6.	______________________	______________________
7.	______________________	______________________
8.	______________________	______________________
9.	______________________	______________________
10.	______________________	______________________

Be Kind

How many times have you noticed someone on the side of the road with a sign asking for money or selling newspapers? In these situations, I never know what to do. Should I give the person money? Is the person really in desperate need? Does it matter? I live an abundant life, so does it matter where the money goes?

For many of us, being charitable is about giving money to worthy causes. That type of giving is a positive and necessary part of being generous, as we all know that many worthwhile organizations wouldn't survive without continuous support. What about the actions you take or don't take toward others on an everyday basis—letting a car get in front of you on the highway, or not beeping the horn when you legitimately could? How about buying what Boy Scouts and ball players are selling, whether cookies or popcorn or raffle tickets?

Think about how many things you do that are random and anonymous. How often do you do them? I recently asked my parents what three pieces of advice they would give their children. I love and am humbled by one of my dad's responses. One of his top three was: "Help others. A good deed is not returned, it is passed on." I know he lives that on a daily basis—he is a great role model for being kind just because it is the right thing to do!

I remember reading a book called *Random Acts of Kindness*. I was inspired to think more consciously about what I was doing to be kind and support those around me. When I searched the Internet to find the book, I came upon the website *helpothers.org*. When you look at the website, you can't help but be inspired to brighten someone's day! Read some of the stories, and see if they make you want to print "smile cards" and start passing them around.

There are many ideas and actions that we could do to positively affect others, and most cost little or no money. On another website, *Lifehack.org*, the author lists twenty-nine ideas for carrying out random acts of kindness every day. In that spirit, here are twenty ideas that you can start doing. I encourage you to try a few or develop your own and, as my dad says, "Pass it on."

1. Buy coffee for a coworker.
2. Find an inspirational passage, and send it to your friends.
3. Send a card to a family member for no reason.
4. Bring something homemade to work.
5. Pick up litter.
6. Spend time with an animal at the Society for the Prevention of Cruelty to Animals (SPCA).
7. Collect books, and bring them to a nursing home.
8. Tell a restaurant manager how good the waiter was.
9. Do something nice for the person at the front desk in your office.
10. Thank the receptionist.
11. Send someone flowers for no special reason.
12. Send money, anonymously, to someone who needs it.

13. Send notes and thank-you cards frequently, personally and professionally.
14. Make it a habit to do one kind act a day.
15. Help someone on the side of the road.
16. Help a mother traveling with small children.
17. Notice people—look them in the eye, and greet them in a friendly manner.
18. Say "thank you."
19. Smile.
20. Put money in someone's parking meter.

Make a commitment to perform at least one random act of kindness before the day is over. I guarantee that you will make someone's day! Make it a habit to do at least one random act of kindness each day.

Random Acts of Kindness List

Remembering to show kindness to those in need not only helps the individual who receives our kindness, it also helps us. Make a list of ways to carry out random acts of kindness every day.

1. ______________________________

2. ______________________________

3. ______________________________

4. ______________________________

5. ______________________________

6. ______________________________

7. ______________________________

8. ______________________________

9. ______________________________

10. ______________________________

11. ______________________________

12. ______________________________

13. ______________________________

14. ____________________

15. ____________________

16. ____________________

17. ____________________

18. ____________________

19. ____________________

20. ____________________

Know That Everything Happens for a Reason

Life is full of disappointments—or is it? We have all experienced not getting a job we wanted or a relationship not working out. Maybe we wished for something that didn't materialize. What are we to make of these disappointments or dreams unrealized? I have long had the mantra, "Everything happens for a reason." Although I believe it is true, learning to have faith in this philosophy has been a hard lesson to learn.

Having dreams and goals are important. I am not suggesting that you sit down and wait for things to happen as if you have no control or responsibility. However, I also believe that you have to have faith that there is something bigger than us at work. There is an even bigger plan, and sometimes we have to trust that it will work out for the best even if it doesn't seem possible at the time. Some events that seemed like my biggest disappointments turned out to be temporary disappointments, and later I realized that those disappointments made room for something even better than I could have imagined.

I recall a time when I didn't get a position I wanted, a relationship failed, or a dream didn't work, no matter how hard I tried. The position was given to someone else when I thought I was more qualified. The relationship ended, and I was devastated. The dream of a happy marriage seemed to elude me. Where am I today? I have a job in another part of the country doing different and interesting work. I found a wonderful man with two children, and we have been married for several years. I could never have known then that things would turn out as they are today, but I am so glad they did.

I believe that it is important to have dreams and goals and to work toward them. I also believe that you need to be open to a better plan. Sometimes that better plan requires being open to an experience or taking a chance. Had I not taken a chance to go on the first date with my husband, my life would be different. Had I not decided to try working in Boston for my first job, my life would be different. There is a great book by Willie Jolley entitled *A Setback is a Setup for a Comeback*, which focuses on what to do when life throws you a curveball.

I recognize there are times when I hold onto a dream or idea way too long and cause myself additional pain and suffering. For example, I had a relationship that I knew was not healthy for me, but I stayed, hoping that things would change. Did they? No. I spent precious time suffering in a bad situation. I may have learned an important life lesson, but I could have been a quicker learner.

A successful life is made up of three components. The first is to have desires, dreams, and goals to go after. Then we must learn from our mistakes and make better decisions going forward, though sometimes we spend a lot of time relearning a lesson we already knew. The last, but most important, component of a successful life is faith—a belief that our future can be full of great surprises and better than we ever imagined. Our job is to work toward our dreams, putting our energy and spirit into achieving those goals. At the same time, we need to be open to the possibility that the next best thing for us may be something we never imagined or will come out of what looked like the worst thing to happen to us.

Today, be open to life—all the twists and turns. Trust that there is a power greater than yourself working to bring good things into your life, and believe that the future is going to be bright.

Overcoming Disappointment

Think about the disappointments you have faced. In many cases, over time, those disappointments show their "silver lining." For example, a failed relationship might make way for a new person to come into your life. List some disappointments that have resulted in something better coming into your life.

	Disappointing Event	Positive Result from the Event
1.	______________________	______________________
2.	______________________	______________________
3.	______________________	______________________
4.	______________________	______________________
5.	______________________	______________________
6.	______________________	______________________
7.	______________________	______________________
8.	______________________	______________________
9.	______________________	______________________
10.	______________________	______________________

Forgive Yourself and Others

The other night, I was watching *What Not to Wear*—it is my version of total indulgence. On the show, there was a woman named Amanda who couldn't forgive herself for failing at a business. Her inability to move on was causing her to feel bad about herself, dress badly, and hide from the world. What was amazing was how different and pretty she looked when she started to give herself positive attention and begin her journey of self-forgiveness.

Today in my daily devotional reading, I read, "I choose to forgive and free myself to move forward." What struck me about these words was the importance of forgiveness to help us move forward. How many of us are stuck in an event, mistreatment, or rejection that happened in the past—in some cases, way in the past? By continuing to dwell on what happened, we allow the situation to continue in the present and affect our lives. As I watched the TV show, it was evident that the effects of the painful event for Amanda had caused her to punish herself for years. Her inability to forgive herself affected those around her as well.

Do you have past hurts that you have not been able to forgive yourself for? How do you learn to forgive yourself or others? First, recognize that forgiveness is a decision to let go of resentment, regret, or thoughts of revenge. It is possible to forgive without minimizing the injustice or wrong. You can still hold others accountable, but forgiveness allows you to move on with your own life.

Why should you forgive? There are many health and emotional benefits to forgiveness:

- Relief from negative emotions such as bitterness
- Increased ability to be compassionate and kind
- Development of healthy relationships
- Physical and psychological health
- Decreased blood pressure, anxiety, and depression

Once you have decided to forgive, make a commitment to change yourself. This can be challenging, especially if you have become comfortable defining yourself by these hurts and feel you were a victim in these situations. If you can't resolve on your own, it may be time for a professional to help you work through the difficult experiences. Sometimes it can help to write the situation or event down in great detail—what happened, how you felt, and how it affects your life today. When you are ready to move on and forgive yourself and others in the situation, take what you wrote, and burn it. There is something powerful and symbolic in burning or destroying the paper—it is permission to let it go. We have all needed forgiveness in our lives. Think about a time when someone forgave you for a wrongdoing. What did the person do? How did it help you move on? Maybe you can apply the same action to the situation you are struggling with.

It is important not to confuse forgiveness with reconciliation. Forgiving someone else or yourself does not imply that you accept the wrongdoing. It allows you to stop living in the past and start living in the present. Forgiveness does not expect change in anyone but you.

Life is lived by moving forward. By not forgiving yourself or others, you hold yourself back from living your life today and in the future. By holding onto resentment, you let a past hurt continue to hurt you today. Make a decision today to let go of any issue that is keeping you from your best life now!

Forgiveness List

Identify five people who you need to forgive.

1. ____

2. ____

3. ____

4. ____

5. ____

If you forgave any or all of the people on the list, what would that change for you? What new behaviors are you going to start, and what behaviors are you going to stop?

____

____

____

____

Overcoming Disappointment: Learn to Bounce Back

Disappointment can come in many forms; it can be career, friendships, a dream, or a goal not attained. If you have been successful so far, you have already experienced a number of setbacks, wrong turns, and defeats. Each time you face disappointment, do you get stronger and more resilient or more bitter and afraid?

I can't remember who said "it doesn't matter how many times you fall down, it's how many times you get up," but it sums up what it means to bounce back from disappointment. To be successful, we need to learn how to respond positively and constructively to disappoints and defeat and see that these setbacks ultimately lead us to success.

The first thing to realize is that disappointment is going to occur. We can do a number of things to avoid failure and disappointment like planning, anticipating, and taking precautions. However, none of these things keep disappointment from ever knocking on our door. Sometimes disappointment comes in spite of our best efforts, and the amount of disappointments we experience is directly related to how high we set our goals and standards. The more we stretch, the more we try—and the more we open ourselves up to experiencing setbacks and difficulties.

If we can't prevent disappointments, what can we control? We can control how we deal with them. Are you the type of person who lets failure stop you from moving ahead, or do you recover and move on?

How can we increase our ability to overcome disappointment and bounce back quickly? Here are a few ideas.

Take some time to adjust to what is. Before we can move forward, we have to accept reality. It doesn't mean we have to like it, but we do have to acknowledge it. If we don't take this step, we will move into denial, which will prevent us from taking positive steps toward our future.

When we are ready, we need to ask ourselves two questions. This idea comes from *Change Your Thinking Change Your Life* by Brian Tracy. The questions are, "What did I do right?" and "What would I do differently?" These questions allow us to glean from the situation what we want to keep doing, because it will help us be successful in the future. It requires us to think through the areas in which we need to behave or think differently to bring about success. In addition to giving us data we can use in the future, it keeps us from taking a blaming point of view. Blaming ourselves or beating ourselves up does little to help us feel better or to motivate us to make behavioral changes.

We can think only one thought at a time, so it is important during periods of disappointment that we guard against negative thinking. It is important to take responsibility for the outcome, but that doesn't mean that we need to continuously beat ourselves up over it. It is appropriate to feel sad or angry, but it is not healthy to stay stuck in these emotions. Move into thinking about the positive aspects of the situation as quickly as possible.

Look at your life in terms of cycles, periods of ups and downs. Look back on your life, and notice other times when you faced adversity or challenges. Do you notice that those difficulties had a lesson in them or positives that came out of bad circumstances? This pattern will repeat itself in the future. Difficulty can bring about new, positive changes.

Resist going into denial. Being in denial keeps us from taking responsibility and from determining a new course of action. We may need some time to recover, but we shouldn't allow it to consume us.

Don't give up too easily, but know when you have given it everything you've got. Many of us fear disappointment and rejection so much that we give up on our dreams too easily. There are countless examples of individuals who "gave it their all" and succeeded at attempt number twenty-eight, sixty, or one thousand. There is no one formula for figuring it out. There is no guarantee that your persistence will pay off. There is no shame in closing the door because you gave it everything you had. The important point is to trust your own compass and not let fear or disappoint shut the door too quickly.

Try gratitude. When it feels like everything is going wrong or we are not making progress on our dreams, it can be hard to notice all the things that are good, right, and a blessing even though they may be right in front of us. There are many good things that that we may be taking for granted. Take a moment to notice all the blessings or lucky breaks you currently have.

Grieve and let go. Sometimes, a dream is going to die. A hope isn't going to be realized, and when that happens, there is loss. It is important to give yourself time to feel the emotions that come with that realization. Take care of yourself. Recuperate, but remember not to fall into despair.

Disappointment is a part of life. We may not choose what those disappointments will be, but we get to choose how we will handle it. If you are facing disappointment today, learn to accept it, and decide what you are going to do to change it and bounce back.

Inspiration to Help You Keep Going

When going after your dreams, you may be tempted to give up with faced with struggles, failure, or adversity. During these times, you need the motivation from others who have overcome similar or greater struggles. Here is a list of famous success stories. You may want to read their biographies to help you stay motivated and focused on going after your own dreams!

Walt Disney
Thomas Edison
Abraham Lincoln
Helen Keller
Winston Churchill
J. K. Rowling
Wilma Rudolph
Henry Ford
Oparh Winfrey
Lucille Ball
Stephan Spielberg
Michael Jordan
Albert Einstein
John Grisham
Dr. Seuss

Who is an inspiration to you, and why?

Be the Best You

We live in a world of comparison. Sometimes, we compare ourselves to "the Joneses"—making comparisons with others whom we think are better off than we are. As a result, at can be hard to figure out what "being the best you" might look like. Determining our best selves will be as unique as each of us and should focus on continuous growth and development. It is a journey, not a destination.

In a recent *Daily Word* devotional reading was a statement that said it all: "Today is a new day in which I can do my best to improve myself and to be the best person I know to be." Based in the number of helpful tips and articles on the Internet, "becoming the best you" is a popular topic.

Why should we strive to be the best version of ourselves? I believe that we should continually develop into who we are created to be, because we all have a unique purpose for being here on earth. For some, our purpose is clear early on. However, I would argue for many, learning their purpose develops over the years. Take J. K. Rowling, for example. She is the author of the Harry Potter book series. Did you know that when she started writing the first novel, she was poor and living on public assistance? What if she believed that was the best her life was ever going to be? She chose to work toward a dream, and in the process, she found her purpose. By continually reaching toward her goal, she changed her life and the lives of many others.

The next question is how we work toward becoming who we were meant to be. Although there are many ways to answer this question, I would like to concentrate on five steps.

1. **Every day, focus on being the best you.** Do you wake up in the morning and consciously think about how you can improve yourself? Focus on projecting the best image of you. Just as we need to continually exercise to stay in shape, we need to focus on developing ourselves to become who we were uniquely designed to be.

2. **Stop comparing yourself to others.** The funny thing about human nature is that we never compare our good fortune to those *less* fortunate. We tend to compare ourselves to others who appear to have more. This comparison leaves us feeling less than and drives us to achieve what we think others have achieved. This is especially true when it comes to material possessions. We need to be careful that we don't measure our worth and our life according to an outside standard. There will always be someone who has more money, more opportunity, etc. Measure yourself based on your growth and contributions to the world. Ask yourself, "Am I continuing to learn and develop? Am I giving back to the world and my family? Am I focusing on friendships and relationships that are important to me?" If you cannot answer with a loud yes, here is where you can start to become a better you.

3. **Take action.** We all have talents that we can develop. Do you know what your unique gifts and passions are, and are you taking steps to develop those areas? J. K. Rowling didn't start out knowing that she was a great writer. She started by taking steps to write. What unique talents do you have, and what are you doing to develop them?

4. **Believe in yourself.** This is perhaps the hardest step if you did not learn this habit as a child. Most individuals who have become successful in their chosen field believed in their dream and themselves. Steven Spielberg and George Lucas had incredible vision and passion for film. They believed in their thoughts and abilities, and look at the results of their work. They made mistakes and learned from them rather than giving up. Oprah Winfrey started her career in news but took a chance when offered a TV talk show. Make a commitment to talk positive about yourself, to yourself, and be determined to learn what makes you unique.

5. **You are a work in progress.** See your life as opportunity to express your talents rather than a chance to fail. Think of yourself as a project in development. Every day gives you chance to become more.

Believing in yourself is critical to living a great life. No matter where you are, life can get better. No matter how old you are, you can achieve your dreams, and no matter what has happened, there is hope in the future. The best gift we can give young people is to encourage them to believe in themselves and provide an example of what that looks like. Today, decide to be the best you, and take steps to move in that direction. It may take you to places that you never dreamed of!

Be the Best You Quiz

Every day, focus on being the best you. What are you going to do daily to be the best you that you can be?

____

____

____

____

Stop comparing yourself to others. Ask yourself these questions daily:

1. Am I continuing to learn and develop?
2. Am I giving back to the world and my family?
3. Am I focusing on friendships and important relationships? If not, why not?

____

____

____

____

What are your unique gifts and talents?

1. ____

2. ____

3. ____

4. ____

5. ____

6. ____

7. ____

8. ____

9. ____

10. ____

Do Something You Are Afraid to Do, Just for Practice

I can proudly say that I have tried hang gliding (I still remember the headache) and rock climbing (another headache), drove on the autobahn, got lost in Germany and found my way (eventually), went on vacation by myself, and joined Toastmasters. All these experiences scared me half to death before I did them, and many of them had me terrified while I was doing them, but I remember the feelings of satisfaction and pride when I completed each activity.

As children, we have to learn to do so many things that trying new things is a part of life. Making mistakes, trying something you have never done, being afraid—all these are part of a child's learning process. Ironically, as we become adults, we can lose the feeling of adventure, or it is replaced with fears of failure, the unknown, and loss.

Susan Jeffers wrote a great book called *Feel the Fear and Do It Anyway*. She talks about moving from saying "I can't" to "I won't," becoming a more positive thinker, and gaining your power back in spite of your fears. The more we face our fears (we probably can't eliminate them) and practice taking steps while being afraid, the more we teach ourselves that we are capable of many things.

Make a list of the things you would do if it weren't for the fear of failure, loss, or looking silly. Now find one thing that you are going to do in the near future. Give yourself a date to accomplish it, and get started.

Just like exercising, keeping fear away requires continuously stretching beyond your comfort zone. You will be amazed at the results you get when you practice doing things you are afraid to do!

My "Afraid To Do" List

1. Make a list of all the things you would do if you were not afraid.

2. Pick one item from the list that you really want to accomplish.

____

____

3. Write down one step that you could take in the next twenty-four hours that would move you closer to accomplishing this goal.

____

____

Let Go of Worry

If I could change one thing about myself, it would be my tendency to worry. A friend of mine recently recalled that her grandmother told her that she would be more than happy to help my friend with her worrying if it would change anything, but if it wasn't going to change anything, she wasn't going to waste the energy. Some people worry more than others, whether they have cause or not. Although I often feel as though I have my life under control, there have been many times when I became physically sick or needed medication to help my worrying. I'm not proud of my response, but it brought about some positive results. For instances, I've introduced tools in my life to help with my worry including yoga, meditation, and reading.

During the recent celebration of my parents' fiftieth wedding anniversary, I found myself talking about this subject with my sister, who is not a worrier. As I watched my parents and thought about their lives, I realized that they have had great lives with lots of great moments and adventures with family and friends. Although there have been difficult times, the good has far outweighed the bad. This led me to think about a friend who recently had serious, life-threatening medical issues and is one of the most grounded and happiest people I know. It makes me wonder why I let little things cause me stress, spending time thinking about the future and fearing the worst. The worst part of worry is that I waste energy fearing events that never happen.

On the website, *westegg.com,* it references the Dale Carnegie's book, *How to Stop Worrying and Start Living. The web author* summarizes the most important points of the book: Don't fuss about small stuff, compartmentalize worry and give it a time limit, don't think about your enemies, and cooperate with the inevitable. Carnegie's book is a great source for ideas in dealing with worry. In addition to Carnegie's techniques, I've compiled several ways to keep worry at bay.

- **Relax!** Regularly participate in a relaxing activity. It needs to be something that allows you to stop thinking for a period of time. It can be physical, like yoga or walking, which has two benefits: strengthening your body while calming your mind. It can be a less rigorous activity, such as listening to meditation tapes, painting, or, in my case, sewing. Most important, find something that you enjoy and that is not a stressor in itself.

- **Take care of yourself.** Pay attention to three important parts of your life—eating, sleeping, and exercising. You can never be at your best if you are not taking care of your body. Good, nutritious food is similar to putting gas in your car. You would never think of putting in water instead of gas, because you would quickly learn that your car wouldn't run properly. If you continuously ignore good nutrition habits, your body will run poorly. Your body needs to rest. If you don't get enough sleep, it is similar to not stopping to change the oil in your car, which will cause engine problems. All of us have heard about the importance of exercising. You need to keep your body in shape if you hope to live a long and healthy life. It is a sad fact that many of us treat our cars better than we treat our bodies. Remember your body needs to last a lifetime.

- **Set reasonable limits.** No more superwoman or superman! Know your physical and emotional limits, and set them. Although it sounds counterproductive, set a limit on how much time you devote to worrying. When you are faced with something that worries you, decide how much time and when you will focus your thoughts on the issue, and refuse to give it any time beyond the allotted period.

- **Count your blessings.** We all have so much for which to be thankful, yet we tend to focus on areas that we are not happy about. Counting our blessings is a way to focus on the positive things we have in our lives, even during difficult circumstances. Writing down what we are thankful for can help us redirect our thinking and get "unstuck" from worrying. It is difficult to be grateful and worry at the same time.

- **Take one day at a time.** In many support groups, they share the concept of concentrating only on the next twenty-four hours, otherwise known as the present. Because none of us know what the future holds—good or bad—it doesn't make sense to spend a lot of time thinking or worrying about it. We can't change the past by dwelling on it either. Both types of thoughts waste the time we have in the present. A better use of time is to effectively use the twenty-four hours that are immediately before us.

This weekend, I was humbled into thinking about how much time and energy I waste and the moments I lose to worry. It is a bad habit that when left unchecked can cause adverse physical symptoms and waste precious time that we can't get back. Decide today to become a "recovering worrier." What actions are you going to take to lessen the time you lose to worrying?

Let Go of Worry List

One way to lessen your worries is to write them down so that you can focus on solutions. Make a list of all the issues you are worried about right now.

1. ______________________________
2. ______________________________
3. ______________________________
4. ______________________________
5. ______________________________
6. ______________________________
7. ______________________________
8. ______________________________
9. ______________________________
10. ______________________________
11. ______________________________
12. ______________________________
13. ______________________________

14.____

15.____

Determine the amount of time to focus on worrying about the items on the list. Your worry time should be no more than fifteen minutes a day. Once you have worried that amount of time, don't allow yourself to worry any more for the reminder of the day. You will notice that you feel more relaxed. You may even free up mental energy to find solutions to those things you are worried about.

Overcome Rejection

What do Walt Disney, Abraham Lincoln, Colonel Sanders, and Norman Vincent Peale have in common? They all overcame rejection and achieved enormous success in their fields.

Bankrupt in the 1930s, Walt Disney's first ideas for the entertainment industry failed. Rather than give up, he moved to Hollywood, where he produced some of the best animated films, gave us our beloved Mickey Mouse, and created family-focused theme parks like Walt Disney World.

Ask any American to name a president, and many will say Abraham Lincoln. However, as well known as he became, he held only one term in the House of Representatives before twice failing to become a senator. With perseverance, he went on to become president during possibly the most difficult era in American history, bringing our country through civil war.

Colonel Sanders founded Kentucky Fried Chicken. His upbringing included running away from home and quitting school in the seventh grade. Although he obtained a successful fried chicken restaurant, he went bankrupt when he was in his forties. He tried to sell his chicken recipe as a franchise business, receiving over a thousand nos before hearing a yes. After such a rocky start, he sold his business in the early 1970s for more than $20 million.

What if these individuals, and countless others who overcame rejection, stopped short of their dreams? Many of you may have great ideas that you aren't pursuing because of fear of rejection, or you tried but didn't meet instant success or positive reactions, so you stopped. You may be tempted to look at those who succeeded and conclude that they were "lucky."

Rejection is difficult, but it is also an important ingredient in achieving your goals. How can you overcome rejection? Here are some things to consider that can help you get past rejection and guide you toward success.

- Learn to view rejection in perspective with life as a whole. Rejection is one person's opinion or one organization's response, and it happens in one space in time. Rather than see rejection as something that is wrong with *you*, see it as not being a fit for "them." For eleven publishers, Norman Vincent Peale's book, The Power of Positive Thinking, wasn't the right fit, but for number twelve, it was an extremely smart and profitable decision. Rejection by a person or organization is an opinion, not a fact, so dust yourself off and move on.

- Learn to look at rejection as data that you can use. When Lincoln was defeated in the race for senator, he could have chosen to stop, but he used the experience to figure out what to improve on so that he could achieve his goal. When receiving feedback, you decide whether or not it is useful.

- Learn from others who have overcome adversity. Bibliographies are a great source of information. They contain stories, wisdom, and inspiration. Most of the time, I find that what moves people to greatness is the ability to never give up and to believe in themselves and their dreams. Walt Disney's desire to build a family-focused getaway inspired him to create a theme park like no other.

- List your good qualities; review the list often, and add to it as you discover new attributes. In the face of rejection, read that list to reinforce your value. I love this quote by Arnold Schwarzenegger: "I knew I was a winner back in the late sixties. I knew I was destined for great things." Now *that* is a way to go through life! That type of thinking helped him to be successful as a weightlifter, actor, and governor. What could you achieve if you adopted this type of thinking?

- Take another step. Rejection can be paralyzing. It can make you afraid, but the worst thing you can do about rejection is nothing. As Walt Disney said, "The way to get started is to quit talking and begin doing." What can you begin doing or changing to become more successful in the future?

- Believe that everything happens for a reason. I think it helps to believe that life is not random. In looking at my own life, I see that even the most painful events had a positive lesson to teach me or that something better came afterward.

Today, think about your dreams and the steps you can take to move toward them. If you are stuck because of rejection, look at your list, pick one step you can take to move forward, and do it.

Overcome Rejection

Learning to overcome rejection is hard. Remember that rejection does not make us a bad or unworthy; it is a situation that isn't right. Many times, something good comes from a bad situation. When we face rejection, we need to determine what action we need to take next to move forward.

If you are facing or have faced an event in your life that is causing you to feel negativity toward yourself, it is time to stop thinking and start acting.

What actions can you take, in the next month, to move forward and start feeling better about yourself?

Timeframe	**Action I Will Take**
Immediately	______________________________
Next twenty-four hours	______________________________
Next week	______________________________
Next month	______________________________

Integrity

Today more than ever, we all need to think about the importance of integrity. I am disheartened by the recent financial crisis, and I find myself thinking that the need for integrity is even more critical in our decisions.

It used to be that a person's word was their bond. How many of us today feel that we can take people at their word, personally or professionally? Our world has changed, and legal documents and written commitments are needed, but have these "cautionary measures" helped or made us less honest and trustworthy? It is sad that we are no longer surprised (or outraged) by the dishonesty of our political and business leaders. What world will we leave our children if we continue on this path?

We all need examples of people and businesses in the world doing things right. I wish there were more examples of businesses setting the example. Johnson & Johnson stands out as a business with integrity by the way it handled the "Tylenol scare" of the 1980s. When Johnson & Johnson discovered that their Tylenol brand had been tampered with, they pulled all Tylenol bottles off the store shelves – even those that they didn't believe where tampered with. The company thought restoring public trust was more important than company profits. Can you point to examples in your life that stand out as great examples of doing the right thing?

Most of us understand, at a high level, what integrity is, and we aspire to do the right thing. The big question is this: "What does it take to live a life in this fashion?" It comes down to doing things consistently and managing to do them when it would be easier, maybe not even noticeable, not to.

Many of us do the right thing on a large scale, but do we cheat when we think it doesn't matter? Think about how you spend the company's money or how truthful you are on your taxes. Do you extend yourself when it's inconvenient, and are you polite and kind when others are not?

The second part of integrity is about being faithful in our words and promises. It used to be that your word was all you needed, but today, many of us feel jaded and that a "promise" isn't worth a lot. Look at all the promises we don't keep to others and ourselves. How many of us are guilty of promising something to our children or spouse that we don't complete until "reminded"? How many of us promise to complete work assignments or requests and justify why we didn't complete them on time? We need to get back to a place where we take our commitments, our words, and ourselves more seriously.

The third part of integrity is the language we use. Today, businesses and governments can be creative with the words they use. As I write this, I think about Janet Jackson's "wardrobe malfunction" at the Super Bowl years ago. Do any of us believe that it was a mistake, an unplanned event? We need to say what we mean,

mean what we say, and say it plainly. This is especially true when it comes to admitting when we were wrong, made a mistake, or failed to do something. Most of us know when we are being fed a line, and yet how many of us are guilty of doing it to someone else? It is painful to admit that we failed or let others down, but they probably already know and sure would appreciate our being direct about it.

The last part of integrity is facing bad news bolding and candidly. It goes hand and hand with saying things directly and plainly. None of us are perfect, and we make mistakes. When we do, the best thing we can do is to admit it and make amends right away. It is humbling to say that we did something wrong and ask for forgiveness, but isn't that what we as parents teach our children so that they can become responsible, mature, conscientious adults? Are we acting as role models of this behavior?

I was taught early in life to "do the right thing," and I strongly believe in this value. I have been tested on it many times, and I am sure I am not done. Sadly, I have failed to uphold this value on many occasions. However, I am convinced that I get it right most of the time, because it's such an important part of who I am that it affects my thought process every day.

Reflect on your own behavior over the last week. Are there times when you didn't act as a role model? We all change the world one action at a time. What can you do to bring more integrity into the world?

Integrity Statements

If integrity is about "doing the right thing," we need to define what that looks like to us on a personal level. What are the commitments we want to make to ourselves about the behavior we want to exhibit? What can others count on us to be true to in "word and deed"?

What are your five integrity statements?

1. ______________________________

2. ______________________________

3. ______________________________

4. ______________________________

5. ______________________________

Over the next week, keep track of how often you act as a role model for the behaviors you listed. Determine what changes you need to make so that you consistently live up to being your best self.

____

____

____

____

Respect Yourself

Respect—it's a word we hear in all areas of our lives. Our military is built on this foundation, and our parents teach us early of its importance. Not only is it important to respect others, we also need to respect ourselves. We start this process by learning to trust our own decisions and thoughts while taking responsibility for them.

Throughout life, there will be people who use their power or confidence to manipulate you toward their ideas, desires, and thoughts. To determine whether someone else's ideas are consistent with yours, you have to first form your *own* opinions, ideas, and preferences. This doesn't mean that you can't change your mind or that you don't have to compromise. It means that you need your own point of view first.

There is a scene in the movie *The Blind Side* where Sandra Bullock's character confronts her friends who are not very supportive of a decision she made. She tells them that she will not continue meeting with them if they can't support her and the decisions that she knows are right for her. Bullock's character is confident of what is right for her and is willing to sacrifice relationships that are counter to what she believes. Unfortunately, many of us worry more about how others will react to our decisions than we listen to our own voice.

There are times where I have interpreted *respect* to mean that I must agree with what others say, even if it contradicts my own beliefs. The frustration I feel when I do this tells me otherwise. I have learned that I can respect others' views without compromising my own.

Think about what is important to you. What ideas, opinions, and points of view do you *know* are significant in your life? What do you value, how do you like to work, and how do you want others to interact with you? Don't be afraid to acknowledge and state your agreement or opposition with others. If you notice that others do not credit you or your ideas, let them know what you need in order to continue with the relationship, conversation, or work project. You will be much more productive if you respect yourself, and it will help others to respect you.

Respect Yourself

If I truly and fully respected myself for the unique individual that I am, I would start:

____

____

____

____

If I truly and fully respected myself for the unique individual that I am, I would stop:

____

____

____

____

Don't Accept Others' Limitations of You

Throughout life, others will try to convince you to think as they do, even if their type of thinking isn't in your best interest. You will have people tell you that your ideas are not good enough or will never work. You will have dreams that don't appear to others to be realistic, so they will try to "protect" you by working to persuade you to give up on those thoughts. You will have people who believe that you can't do something and will spend a lot of time telling you not to try. Don't take any of the chatter to heart.

Overcoming rejection and not accepting others' limitations of you are related concepts. Rejection can be the primer that starts you down the path of seeing yourself in a negative way, but *accepting* others' limitations of you goes further. It means that you accept others' opinions more than you trust your internal voice.

Many of us have bought into the thinking that if we reach a level of success (however you define success), the criticizing will stop, and we will gain acceptance from others. I would argue that although success does bring acceptance, it also invites more criticism. No matter what you do in life, you won't be able to please everyone; so the sooner you stop trying to achieve this impossible standard, the saner your life will be.

Each of us has an inner voice; it's that gut feeling that lets you know that something is right for you. That voice may be telling you to take a risk and experience something new, or it may be the desire to learn something new. Each of us has goals and dreams that are unique to us, but many of us silence those thoughts as soon as someone tells us that they disapprove.

The other day I read an article in *More* about a woman who is my new hero. Kathryn Stockett is the author of *The Help*, which has become a bestseller and a movie. In the article, she tells how her book was rejected sixty times before it was published. Those sixty rejections didn't stop her from pursuing her dream; they fueled her dream. Rather than letting go of her desire to get her book published, she continued to work at her writing. With each rejection, she went back and rewrote the book, making it a little better. Sometimes rejection can paralyze you, making it difficult to take the next step, but this was not the case with Stockett. She didn't accept the views of others as the final word on her dream. She continued to believe in herself and to submit her book to other agents. She believed in her own voice as a writer and believed that she was worthy of being published. Today, she is a sought-after writer!

Dreams + action + belief in yourself = success

We are blessed with countless examples of people who exhibit this type of faith, hope, and optimism and the amazing achievements they produce. They are not more talented than you are, but they may listen to better voices.

Today, take Stockett's example, and take back the power you have given to others. Put others' views in their appropriate place: something to be considered but not something that overrules your own beliefs.

What dreams been placed on a shelf because someone criticized or rejected them? What actions and improvements could you take to develop your dream? Today, commit to taking one action toward fulfilling your dreams.

Don't Accept Others' Limitations of You

Identify one dream that is important to you:

____

____

Identify one action you can take now that will move you closer to your dream:

____

____

What do you need to change about your thinking or actions to increase your belief in yourself?

____

____

Repeat daily.

Dealing with Difficult People

We have all had to deal with difficult people. Maybe they are the coworkers who know it all or the bosses who assume that a job title gives them the right to treat others badly. Maybe it is the driver who can't be courteous. Bob Sutton, a professor at Stanford University, wrote a bestseller, *The No Asshole Rule,* that focuses on the damage these individuals do to the workplace and employee morale. The devastating effect goes beyond work and spills into our personal lives. Worst yet, we have a tendency to learn from these individuals, and over time, we can begin to act like them.

If you have had to deal with this type of individual, you know what he or she acts like and may have the scars to prove it. Although there are many different types of behavior that can negatively affect others, some are more common than others: claiming power at the expense of others, being self-absorbed, or any of the other "dirty dozen" behaviors Sutton mentions in his book. Unfortunately, we are probably good at recognizing these behaviors in others, but we ignore them in ourselves.

If someone is being difficult, what do you do? In the past, you may have asked someone else to confirm that your hurt is valid, but this knowledge does not change the individual or his or her behavior. A more effective way to deal with difficult people is to recognize that *you* have to change and develop effective coping strategies. Although it may seem unfair that you have to change, it's important that the person affected has to be the first to change, at least in the short term.

What can we do to cope with this type of behavior and minimize our own frustration? In Sutton's book, he highlights several strategies. I would like to focus on three of them.

- **Develop an attitude of indifference.** For many, this is a difficult task, especially for those individuals who believe in fairness, teamwork, and the importance of The Golden Rule. Sadly, the inconsiderate person doesn't operate from the same mindset. Developing a detached attitude lowers your reaction to their behavior and helps you to maintain a sense of equilibrium. By learning to be indifferent to negative behavior, you lessen the chances that you will begin to act in the same way.

- **Limit your exposure.** I have used this strategy with great success. I employ it after I have exhausted all other attempts to influence another person to be a positive team member. If I do not have the authority to change the behavior, I move to limited contact.

- **Hope for the best, prepare for the worst.** This strategy does two things. It prevents you from becoming bitter or acting like your offender by reinforcing your belief in your value system. It requires you to anticipate a negative response and be prepared. By doing so, you will not be caught off guard or disappointed, and you will be better prepared to cope with whatever behavior you have to deal with.

We all need to be careful about who we associate with, because we can be influenced by their conduct and attitude. What do we need to be mindful of so we don't develop the same bad behaviors? I'd like to highlight two more from Sutton's book.

- **Focus on ways that you are no better or worse than others.** In our culture, we have many comparisons and a large dose of competitiveness. These attitudes can lead us to compare and compete against others in unhealthy ways. Believing that we are better because we graduated from a particular college or drive a particular car doesn't make us better human beings. Look for commonality and ways to connect with others, especially those who may seem different.

- **Be careful with positional power.** If you have power through title, money, or association, make sure that you are not using it to treat others unfavorably. Being a vice president doesn't give you the right to treat another person disrespectfully. Humiliating, belittling, ignoring, or acting as if you are more important are all disrespectful.

Every day there are more examples of individuals acting in ways that range from inappropriate to downright mean. We may ourselves have acted in ways that haven't shown respect or kindness. Is it the ticket agent's fault that the plane is delayed? Does she or he deserve our wrath? We all need to look in the mirror and make sure that we are not demonstrating bad behavior. If we have to deal with a difficult individual, we need to take steps to minimize the effects of their behavior on ourselves.

I suggest that we all think about how we affect those around us. Are we role models for positive behavior, or are there individuals who say that we are difficult at best and downright jerks at worst? Make a commitment today to try new strategies for dealing with difficult people or becoming less difficult yourself.

Dealing with Difficult People Quiz

Who in my life is a difficult person?

____

____

What can I do to create an attitude of indifference?

____

____

Do I feel I am better or worse than others? How?

____

____

What can I do to change my thinking?

____

____

Are there times that I have justified my behavior based on how others act rather than follow my own guidelines for appropriate behavior?

____

____

Living a Life With No Regrets

As long as I can remember, I have wanted to live a life with no regrets. That isn't to say that I haven't made mistakes or wished that I had done some things different, but I never want to feel like I wished I had or hadn't done something. So far, I have few regrets about things I wish I hadn't done. Although I don't want to repeat some of the experiences, most have taught me valuable lessons.

The type of regret I worry about the most is not experiencing new things. We miss special moments, realizing that we not spending enough time with the special people in our lives or are afraid to go after our dreams. These regrets can feel far worse than any mistake we might make.

It is easy to get used to our routines and responsibilities. As adults and especially as parents, we have a lot of responsibilities, but sometimes we forget to try new things, go to new places, or learn something new. When we are young, we are more willing to try new things—the world is our oyster. As we take on more responsibilities, we tend to lose our need, ability, or desire to experience unfamiliar activities. When was the last time you tried something new? Trying something new can range from trying different foods, learning a new activity, or traveling to a new place. Not long ago, after a lot of asking from my husband, I tried waterskiing. I didn't get up on the skis, at least not for long. Although that might look like a failure, I was having fun, and it was exciting to try. We need to make these types of experiences a regular part of our routine. It keeps life from getting too predictable, safe, or rigid. It is how we stay young and enjoy all that life has to offer.

It is important to celebrate the special moments and even the everyday moments. Many moments in our life are once-in-a-lifetime events, but most of the time, we don't notice them, because they are a part of our everyday experience. There are also those big, special moments that we need to make sure we don't miss. My mother gave my grandparents a fiftieth anniversary party. At the time, it seemed like the right thing to do for such an important milestone. She didn't know that my grandfather would die unexpectedly that fall. It was the last time we were together as a family. The lesson from this life-changing event is that although life is busy and we may be spread apart by geography; we should make time for special moments with those we care about.

When I remember the song "Cat's in the Cradle," I think it is a good metaphor for how life is. My own children will be starting out on their own lives soon. The kids are in there twenties and while they start making their own lives, and it is hard as a parent to let them go. There are the adult relationships that we develop or don't develop with our siblings and our changing roles as our parents' age. Life goes by fast. We need to make sure that we are taking steps to reach out to those who are important to us and cultivate our relationships. If we have a strained or troubled relationship, we need to work on it, if it is an important one. We never know how long we have in this world, and regret is a terrible thing to live with.

The last place where regret can make an entrance is around our dreams. According the website, *Addicted2Success.com*, the number one regret of nursing home patients about their lives is they wished they had pursued their dreams and aspirations. How many of us are doing our dream job or living out our dreams? I am not suggesting that you leave your job tomorrow or sell all your possessions, but I am asking you to get in touch with those deep desires and think about how you might achieve them. It may take many steps to reach your dream, but if you don't start taking the steps, you are guaranteed not to reach it. Make a wish list, and include your smallest wishes, biggest wishes, and wildest wishes. Look at it regularly, and determine what steps to take to make progress toward your dreams. Sometimes a dream comes true because of many small steps that add up. In other cases, it is serendipity. Either way, it is about not letting life go by and living it to the fullest.

Today, make a couple of lists. List the individuals who are important to you and that you want to stay in touch with. Make a commitment to reach out to one person each week with a card, letter, or phone call. Make is a list of all your wishes. Think about one or two goals that you can work on, and start taking those steps. These two lists will change your life—I guarantee it.

Living a Life With No Regrets

List all the people in your life who are important.

____________________	____________________
____________________	____________________
____________________	____________________
____________________	____________________
____________________	____________________
____________________	____________________
____________________	____________________
____________________	____________________
____________________	____________________
____________________	____________________
____________________	____________________
____________________	____________________

Highlight the people that you want to strengthen your relationship with or that you haven't been as connected to as you would like.

Determine what actions you will take, in the next week, to reach out to one person on the list.

I will reach out to ________________________________ and

____ in the next week.

Go back to page 5 and look at the dreams you wrote down. What is one step you could take to move towards achieving one of your dreams?

____

____

Do the Right Thing

My role model for doing the right thing has always been my father. As far back as I can remember, I heard, "If everyone jumped off a bridge, would you?" Quickly translated, it means, "Do what is right, not just what everyone else is doing." I don't think my dad is perfect, but he has set the bar high.

As a manager of people and a mother to two young adults, I believe it is important to set an example and do the right thing. I have noticed that it is not difficult to figure out, just hard to execute. As a leader, I don't believe I can ask others to do something that I am not willing to do. I know that I need to show my children how to make those difficult decisions. If I don't model this, how will they learn?

I try to follow the Five Dollar Principle. If you and I agreed to split a prize equally, and the prize was five dollars, we would do it immediately. We wouldn't even think about it; we would do the right thing and split the money. Why does it become harder when the "prize" is $10,000, $100,000 or $1 million?

I work hard to follow The Golden Rule, treat everyone well, and be gracious and polite. Why is does that become so hard when someone is being rude or self-centered? Why is there "road rage" today and not twenty years ago? It takes a lot of discipline to do the right thing when those around you do not appreciate it, notice it, or repay it with unkindness. These thoughts keep me coming back to "do the right thing":

1. Remember those bumper stickers that said, "What would Jesus do?" For me, it is "What would my dad do" and would he be proud of my behavior?

2. You never know when you are going to influence someone; especially your children, and you need to be an influence for good and be a role model for others.

3. I worry about what kind of a world the next generation will be living in if we don't stop and do the right thing. Who will help those who can't help themselves such as the poor, animals, or the environment?

By doing the right thing, we contribute to the collective good and may make a difference in someone's life, a difference that may affect the person in a significant way. You never know.

Are you doing the right thing in all parts of your life? If not, what do you need to change?

Do the Right Thing Quiz

Who or what needs my help?

____

____

____

____

If I were a role model for doing the right thing, what behaviors would I engage in?

____

____

____

____

If I were a role model for doing the right thing, what behaviors would I **not** engage in?

____

____

____

____

Learn to Ignore the Joneses

If asked, many of us might have a difficult time admitting to our desire to keep up with those we admire and who we believe are doing better economically and socially. This desire to "keep up with the Joneses" has been the subject of American culture since the 1950s.

Financial advisor and author Dave Ramsey reminds us that the "Joneses" are broke, and who wants to be broke?

Do you tend to compare yourself to what you see on the "outside" of others' lives? Do you know if your comparison is accurate and those you are comparing yourself to are financially solid, or do they just look like they have a lot of money?

According to a May 2012 *Forbes* article, the average household credit card debt is $6,772, which translates into a lifestyle built on borrowed money. Even more frightening is the statistic from the Federal Reserve Board, which estimates that 43 percent of Americans spend more than they earn.

Authors Thomas J. Stanley and William D. Danko studied millionaires over a thirty-year period and shared their results in their book, *The*

Millionaire Next Door. They revealed some surprising discoveries about millionaires, such as the fact that most millionaires keep their cars for up to ten years, live in modest homes, and tend to shop at discount stores like Walmart. While I am not implying that shopping at Walmart will make you a millionaire, I am suggesting that holding onto your money is the way to acquiring wealth.

It is hard to ignore "the Joneses." Advertisers tell you that they are happier and have more friends. Stores lead you to believe that you can live that lifestyle if you buy whatever gadget or item they sell. In a culture that is in love with brand names, learning to change your thinking can be challenging, but if the Joneses are secretly broke, do you *really* want to be like them?

How do you know if you are trying to keep up with the Joneses?

- ➢ Do you have any credit card debt?
- ➢ Are you living in a house that you didn't put at least 10 percent down on when you bought it because you couldn't afford to do so?
- ➢ Do you desire to have a sports car, SUV, or other trendy car because you noticed that someone else had one?
- ➢ Have you ever bought a TV, computer, or boat on credit?
- ➢ Do you feel better about yourself and more successful when you wear specialty clothing?
- ➢ Do you buy items on credit most of the time because you can't wait to get them?

If you said yes to any of these questions, you may want to consider your purchasing habits and whether you're trying to keep up with a certain, and possibly unrealistic, standard of living.

Ignoring the Joneses is hard, but it can be done. Here are some things you can do to get out of this cycle of trying to live up to others' expectations or definitions of success and start defining it for yourself.

1. Determine the areas where you are vulnerable to advertisers or others' opinions, whether it's clothing or cars.

2. Get rid of credit card debt. Make a commitment to stop using credit cards and develop a plan to pay off any balances once and for all.

3. Become a disciplined saver. Have money taken out of your paycheck, or put money in an envelope every week. Commit to not buying things until you can pay for them with cash.

4. Define what success is for you. It is important to realize what you consider success to be and to be honest about it. Material success isn't usually what everyone is after as much as it is about what it represents.

5. Shop less. Commit to going shopping once a week or every other week, or determine to buy clothes once a month. Take that extra money and pay off debt or save it for an emergency.

Our struggle to keep up with the Joneses is creating longer work days and less time with people who are important to us. It creates a false sense of what really matters and increases our attachment to material items.

Reflect on your spending habits, and do a reality check. Determine the areas in which you may be trying to keep up with the

Joneses. Make a commitment to stop trying to live up to an advertiser's standard of success, and define what success looks like to you. If you need more help to get your financial house in order, I highly recommend Ramsey's book *The Total Money Makeover.* The simple but true wisdom in this book can help change your finances forever.

Learn to Ignore the Joneses Quiz

Do you have credit card debt? If yes, why?

___

___

Who do you admire and why?

___

___

What decisions or behaviors do you engage in that stem from a comparison with someone else?

___

___

When do you feel the most successful?

___

___

When do you feel the **least** successful?

___

___

What is the one change you can make now to stop competing with others?

____

____

Learn to Enjoy Work

Another Monday starts. Are you one of those people who can't wait to start another week, or are you hoping that you will be the next Megabucks winner? The book *Happy* by Ian K. Smith, MD, is full of information about being happy. Given that most of us spend the majority of our time at work, maybe that is a good place to start thinking about being happy.

Among the many ideas and tips in the book, Smith suggests five things you can do to enjoy work more:

i. Set goals.
ii. Have fun.
iii. Find something you like.
iv. Remember that you are more than your job.
v. Take a break.

Previously, I mentioned the importance of goals. I think that having goals separates those who feel satisfied from those who don't feel positive about their work and personal life. Do you have goals for yourself for this year? If not, why not? Before you know it, an entire year has gone past. Are you taking steps to make sure that you are using your time wisely and achieving the life you want?

If you have not set any goals for the year, stop now, and set them. Start with five, and make sure that they include both professional and personal goals. (You may want to go back to page 13 and re-read the section on Goals.)

Next is learning to have fun. Children know how to have fun. They spend a lot of time enjoying the company of others, being creative, and exploring. Isn't it a shame that as we get more responsibility, we tend to forget how to have fun. We can be responsible and have fun, and we should make sure to have fun at work and at home. Make it a point to do something fun at least once a week. Make sure that you bring fun into your work environment. You can take the work seriously without taking yourself too seriously. Remember, it's important to laugh often for your physical and mental health.

Do you know what types of activities you enjoy or find relaxing? How often to you do them? My guess is probably not often enough. I love to sew, and it relaxes me. However, when life is busy, it is one of the first things I give up. I need to protect some time so that I have a fun, relaxing activity to look forward to. This is especially true when you have children; make sure that you relax so that they can learn to have fun with you.

The other day, one of my colleagues remarked that he was working a sixty-hour week and said it as if that made him more of a hero than the rest of us who were trying to balance work and home. It made me feel sad for him. I believe that it is important to do well at work. I work hard at my job; but I have learned that there is more to life than work and I am more than my job. When you lose sight of this, you forget to set limits on your workload and work day. Something will suffer. Your body and mind need rest, and if you are working all the time, you don't get enough sleep. The people in your life suffer too. They don't get to see you, or when they do, you are too tired or stressed to be much fun to be around. Make sure to find a balance between work and life.

I would love to be one of those people who takes a day off a week to rest, a weekend off a month to relax, and a week off a quarter to have fun, but I'm not there yet. I take vacations, but they are usually full of activity, and the last time I took a whole weekend off, I was sick. I know it is important and needed if I am to achieve all that I want to. One of my goals for this year is to take Sundays off—just relax and do fun things, no chores or errands. I'm not there yet, but I am working on it.

What changes do you need to make to be happy? Do you have enough fun in your life, professionally and personally? If not, what steps will you take to change this? For today, focus on one area of your life. Think about one activity that you could start doing to bring more happiness into your life, and just do it!

Learn to Enjoy Work Quiz

My five goals are:

1. ______________________________

2. ______________________________

3. ______________________________

4. ______________________________

5. ______________________________

For fun, I like to:

____

____

____

____

I want more relaxation in my life. I plan to make the following change, within the next week, to dedicate more of my time to relaxing.

____

____

____

Be Grateful

On the easy days, I would say I am a grateful person. I consider myself kind, generous and, in general, someone I would describe as a good person. Of course, this is easy when everything is going well. What grade would I give myself on a not-so-easy day?

I believe that everything happens for a reason. Sometimes, I don't know the reason for years, but I don't believe that life is random. I also believe *in life lessons.* If you put these together, you get events and experiences because there is some meaning or learning for you to experience. In *Gratitude: Affirming the Good Things in Life,* in additional to teaching the importance of goal setting, Beattie also inspires us to be grateful for the aspects of our life whether we consider it good or bad.

I know intellectually that I have so much to be thankful for, personally and professionally. Why don't I go around with a positive attitude all the time? Sometimes, I think I let negative thinking take hold. It's easy to find others who have more or seem to have it easier. Do I ever think about how much more fortunate I might be than others?

Gratitude can be cultivated, and it can be developed starting now, regardless of where you are in life. It's about focus. The more we focus on something, the bigger is gets. Developing more gratitude is about noticing and focusing on the positive things. Sometimes it can be hard. You have to start where you are, and if there is a lot going against you, you have to start small. For most of us, there is much to be grateful for: our jobs, our health, where we live, and our families.

Developing an attitude toward gratitude is like building a muscle. It takes practice. Here's something you can do today, and it requires only a pen and piece of paper. Start a list of all the things you are grateful for; set a goal to write between twenty-five and one hundred. To help you build a continuous attitude of gratitude, start each morning by thinking of at least ten things you are grateful for. Do this for sixty days, and see if you feel more grateful and notice more to be grateful about.

Be Grateful

Today, I Am Grateful For:

1. ____
2. ____
3. ____
4. ____
5. ____
6. ____
7. ____
8. ____
9. ____
10. ____
11. ____
12. ____
13. ____

14. ____

15. ____

Complete a Grateful List each day for thirty days, and see if it helps you feel more grateful and positive throughout the day.

Reach Out to Someone

When I was in my twenties, I realized that I had lost touch with my grandmother. As a child, I visited her often and saw her on special occasions. I realized that it had been a while since I had reached out to her. My grandfather had died years earlier, and she lived on her own in Florida. I was busy starting out in my career and involved with my own life, but still it bothered me.

I realized that if anything happened to my grandmother and I didn't reach out to her, I would feel terrible. With that thought in mind, I wrote the first letter I had ever written to her. When I went on a trip, I made sure to send a postcard to her. Every so often, I sent her a "care package" with pictures from the family, stamps, and candy (her favorite treat).

The letters turned into making a trip every year or two to see her in Florida. I took her to the beach and to dinner and watched the shows she liked to watch. I did this for more than twenty years, and I was lucky enough to have my grandmother in my life until she was ninety-three.

When I visited her, I saw all the postcards I sent, because she saved them and proudly displayed them on her cabinets. Not only was I taken aback by how many places I had been to and forgotten, but it made me realize how important those cards were to her. My grandmother lived alone for more than fifteen years, and when she died, my aunt thanked me for writing to my grandmother. She told me how much my grandmother looked forward to getting mail from me.

I am the fortunate one. I had the chance to get to know my grandmother as an adult. I had the chance to make her days a little more joyful and let her know that she was loved and special.

I was extremely sad when she died, but I was at peace knowing that I had made a difference in her life, the way she made a difference in my life when I was younger.

At this stage of my life, I find myself busy again, but I know there are people in my life that I should take the time to reach out to. It is time to send a note or letter, mail the latest pictures of the family, or send a postcard, care package, or unexpected, thoughtful item.

There are people in your life who need to know that they are cared for right now, that someone is thinking of them. Who are those people?

Today, start a list of the people that you would like to reach out to more often, and decide to reach out to one person a month. You will be amazed at how good it will make you feel, and you will be making a difference in someone else's life, sometimes more than you will ever know!

Reach Out to Someone

List ten people who are important to you.

1. ______________________________

2. ______________________________

3. ______________________________

4. ______________________________

5. ______________________________

6. ______________________________

7. ______________________________

8. ______________________________

9. ______________________________

10. ______________________________

List all the things you could do to let them know you care.

____

____

____

____

Pick at least one item from your list that you will do this week.

____

____

____

____

Leverage Your Time

I come from a family of "doers." Get my parents and myself in a room, and we could put the Energizer Bunny to shame. Getting things done has never been an issue, but getting to everything, using my time wisely, and not being stressed out —that is another story. I believe there is truth to the saying, "If you need to get something done, ask a busy person." I think it is true because busy people employ a number of tactics to get things accomplished and like the feeling that comes from completing things. However, there can be a tendency to continue to do more, no matter how unrealistic the timeframe.

With the invention of so many timesaving devices, it is funny we didn't get more time, we actually do more! I don't see the devices going away, and I don't see the workload ceasing, so what are we to do if we don't want to burn out or miss all the important moments of our lives?

My first suggestion isn't going to be popular, but there is mounting research to support it. We need to stop multitasking. Our brains are not wired to do multiple tasks at the same time, at least not important ones. One task, or in most cases both tasks, will suffer. The consequences can be life threatening. Have you ever watched someone try to drive and text at the same time?

Changing this habit for some of us is going to take some practice, so start small. Try making one habit change, and notice the effect on your performance or stress level. I try to refrain from using the cellphone while driving. I can easily justify what a good use of my driving time it would be. I could get a few more items crossed off my list, but I have noticed that my driving ability decreases if I concentrate on the conversation while also trying to drive. What multitasking habit do you need to break?

My second suggestion is write things down and keep them all in the same place. A couple of years ago, I attended a seminar, led by author Dave Allen's company, called "Getting Things Done." I learned a lot in the class and highly recommend his books. One of the nuggets that hit home was the notion that our brain continues to remind us of a task and will take up "mental energy" until the reminder is put where our brain knows that it will be remembered. I have been a list maker most of my life, but without a list to follow, I won't accomplish even 25 percent of what I normally do. I keep pads of paper in my car, in my purse, on my desk, and by the bed, so when an idea comes, I can capture it right away. I put it on a master list that helps me keep track of my professional and personal "to-do" items. I review the list and determine what I need to focus on that day.

My third suggestion comes from a well-known motivational speaker, Zig Ziglar. His observation is that the days right before we go on vacation tends to be our most productive. We know that we need to get certain items accomplished before we leave, and we concentrate with laser-like focus to get those tasks done. His suggestion is to work that way every day. Pretend we were about to go on vacation, and attack our work with the concentration, focus, and determination that we have when we are actually getting prepared for a vacation.

"Take a break" is the fourth suggestion. Our working world today is much different from even five years ago as technology has changed how, when, and where we work. Our work lives and personal lives have become more blurred. We have more activities and commitments to get to for our kids and ourselves. We can do tasks at our decks, at all hours of the day and night, which wasn't possible before the Internet. We have become a supercharged, on-the-go society. We used to eat at the table, as a family gathering together. Today, companies try to devise foods that don't need utensils—can that be a good thing? We aren't getting enough sleep, enough exercise, or even enough fresh air. Our bodies and minds need downtime; if we don't have it regularly, we get stressed or sick and, in most cases, are less effective. The busier we are, the more we need to plan for a break. Pick one activity that you really like, and make sure that you do it at least once a week. Doctor's orders!

The last suggestion is to make sure that you spend your time on what really matters. Most of us do not give ourselves a reality check until something traumatic or tragic happens. If a significant other leaves us, we have a health issue, or we lose a loved one, it causes us to reevaluate where we are spending our energy and time. Are we living our lives in a balanced way, focusing on all the important aspects of life: health, relationships, personal pursuits, and giving back to the world? If the answer is no to any area, we need to look at where we spend our time and make adjustments.

Today, determine your most pressing issue around time. Are you trying to do too many things at the same time? Are you continually forgetting important tasks or assignments? Are you managing your time, or is life managing you? Whatever your pain points, decide today to take one step forward and leverage your time for a better life.

Leverage Your Time List

Keeping track of the many "to dos" you have is an important step in leveraging your time. If you don't have a master to-do list and personal and professional to-do lists, start there. Making a list and keeping it current will minimize stress, increase productivity, and keep you from missing important items. I use the to-do list below for personal actions. You can visit my blog at *melissasbetterworld.com* to get a downloadable copy that you can personalize.

Personal To-Do List—Saturday

Groceries	Important Dates (birthdays, activities)
Shopping	Finances
Special Occasions	Important Events This Week
Errands	Contact
Follow Up	Additional Items

Lessons from Lager

I was lucky to have a dog named Lager. He was eighty-five pounds of pure chocolate lab love. He loved everything and everyone, and he figured that everyone and everything felt the same about him. I was blessed to have Lager in my life for fourteen years, and in those years, he taught me a lot of lessons about how to approach life.

The purpose of my blog, and the goal of this book, is to help others live a better life. I truly think that you can find wisdom in a lot of places, even your pets. Read on, and see if there is anything from the statements below that you want to try in your own life, or just have fun and enjoy the statements.

Life Lessons from Lager

Enjoy the simple things.
Care deeply.
Believe that you are likable, and expect others to like you.
Let others know that you love them as often as possible.
Enjoy the ride.
See life as an adventure, and be open to new experiences.
Run, romp, and play daily.

Thrive on attention, and let people be close to you.
Avoid biting, but stand your ground.
Share what you have whether that is dinner, a toy,
or even a treat.
Show good manners when around others.
Be loyal.
Be particularly gentle with children.
Don't let others make a fool out of you.
Never be too old to learn a new trick.
Never use your size to push those smaller than you around.
Never pretend to be something you're not.
When someone is having a bad day, be silent, sit close by, and
kiss him or her gently.
Play often.

Smile!
Enjoy every moment of every day!
Be happy!

Keep Going

As the famous saying goes, "It isn't how you start that matters, it is how you finish." I am confident that if you picked up this book and have read it, you are looking for ways to make your life better. I believe that one of the most important decisions you can make is to believe that your life can always improve, even if you are living a great life already.

"Living a better life is about balance," as my dad would say. To have a good life, pay attention to all aspects of your life. This includes your health, finances, emotional well being, relationships, and career/work. It also means taking time to think about what makes you unique and what your purpose is here on earth. Maybe you have one general purpose like "making a difference," or maybe you are meant to teach or influence children, to give them hope and a future. Knowing your purpose will help you make sure that you are living a great life.

I hope the articles and ideas in this book have helped you to start thinking about the changes you might want to make, and I hope that this book has confirmed that some of the steps you have taken are the right ones to work toward a great life.

Recently, my family has been dealing with a life-threatening illness of a family member. It came as a surprise—no warning, no symptoms. The person was fine one day, didn't feel good the next, and before we knew it, she wasn't given much hope for a recovery. Not only is it difficult to be a part of this type of experience; it is humbling. Most of us will live long, healthy lives, but we are not guaranteed that. Many of us waste our days thinking that we have a long future ahead and that we will be able to stop and enjoy life or make changes later. That isn't a smart way to go through life. It is my sincerest desire that the ideas in this book have helped you to think about what you need to do to live a better life, and it is my sincerest hope that you will start *now* to take action to live *your best life*!

If you would like more ideas about living your best life, see the Recommended Reading section on the next page. Visit my blog at melissasbetterworld.com, where you will find all types of ideas, suggestions, and articles on a variety of subjects that will help you in all aspects of your life.

Good luck, and enjoy!

Recommended Reading

Emotional Management

Beattie, Melody. *Gratitude: Affirming the Good Things in Life* . MJF Books, 1992.

Carnegie, Dale. Dale Carnegies's Lifetime Plan for Success: How to Win Friends & Influence People and How to Stop Worrying & Start Living. Galahad Books, 1998.

Horn, Sam. *What's Holding You Back*. St. Martin's Press, 1997.

Jeffers, Ph.D., Susan. *Feel the Fear and Do It Anyway.* Random House, 1987.

Jolley, Willie. *A Setback is a Setup for a Comeback*. St. Martin's Press, 1999.

Wiseman, Richard. *The Luck Factor: The Four Essential Principles.* Hyperion, 2003.

Life Management

Bender, Sue. *Plain and Simple*. HarperCollins, 1989.

Pausch, Randy. *The Last Lecture*. Hyperion, 2008.

Time Management

Allen, David. *Getting Things Don*. Penguin Books, 2001.

Covey, Stephen R. *The 7 Habits of Highly Effective People*. Fireside, 1989.

Tracy, Brian. *Time Power. AMACOM, 2007.*
Tracy, Brian. Goals. Berrett-Koehler Publishers, 2003.

Money Management

Clason, George S. *The Richest Man in Babylon*. Penguin, 1988.
Bryant Quinn, Jane. *Smart and Simple Financial Strategies for Busy People*. Simon & Schuster, 2006.
Ramsey, Dave. *The Total Money Makeover* . Thomas Nelson, 2009.
Stanley PhD, Thomas J. and William D. Danko, PhD, *The Millionaire Next Door: The Surprising Secrets of America's Wealthy*, Longstreet Press, 1996.

www.ingramcontent.com/pod-product-compliance
Lightning Source LLC
LaVergne TN
LVHW010923110826
845149LV00013B/2458

* 9 7 8 0 9 8 8 5 5 4 7 0 2 *